PIRATE
Puzzles

Written by Simon Tudhope
Designed by Gregor Laird
and Marc Maynard

Illustrated by Mattia Cerato,
Laurent Kling, Emi Ordás,
Mark Ruffle and Rémy Tornior

Circle the pile of parts that will make a whole cannon.

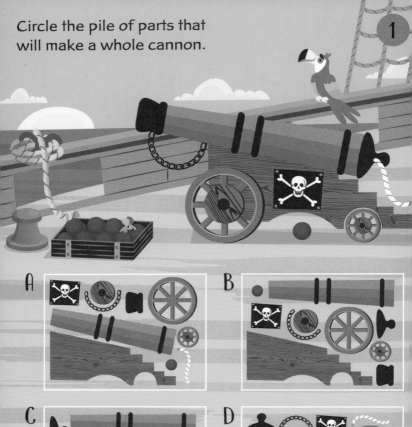

Find the pirate words below in the grid.

```
T E F T B A R Y K
R D N O N N A C O
E N O R I D E L O
A A V R S R U E H
S L E A W T L R G
U S W P O X P R K
R I I E R J O A C
E H A V D Q P B M
S K U L L T E D P
```

TREASURE   BARREL
SHIPWRECK   SKULL
HOOK   ISLAND
CANNON   SWORD
MAP   PARROT

Find the marooned pirate a route to the village that avoids all the sharks.

Fill in the blank labels so that each barrel shows the sum of the two beneath it.

Turn SALT into GOLD by changing one letter at a time. The letters at each stage must form a real word.

S	A	L	T
		L	
S			
	O		
B			
G	O	L	D

Number the pictures in the order they happened.

6

Draw on the blank coins so that every row and column has one of each design.

There's a 20% discount on all the items below, but the price tags haven't been changed yet. Redbeard has 200 pieces of silver. Does he have enough to buy everything on his list?

Shopping list

2 lamps   1 parrot
1 globe   3 compasses
3 hooks   2 hats

20 pieces

35 pieces

25 pieces

5 pieces

50 pieces

20 pieces

35 pieces

15 pieces

10 pieces

2 pieces

Which rope should the pirate pull to find the message hidden in the bottle?

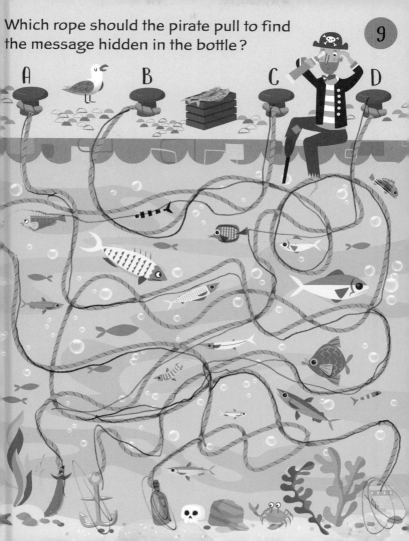

Can you find Brownbeard's parrot? It's the one that isn't part of a matching pair.

Circle the ship that's the same as the one silhouetted against the moon.

Follow the instructions to find the hidden treasure.

Go north if you meet mermaids.

Go east if you meet dolphins.

Follow whales south.

Go west to escape sharks.

Circle the location below where you find the treasure.

Beneath the wreck

Near the temple

Inside the cave

Start here

Using the clues, fill the X-shape with four words ending with 'D' that all have four letters.

Clues:
1. Pirates put this in a chest
2. A parrot is one of these
3. Makes a ship move
4. Pirates bury treasure in

Circle eight differences between these two pictures.

Each item below stands for a different number from 1 to 4. The numbers at the edges of the grid are the sum of the numbers in each row or column. Figure out which item stands for which number and write the answers below.

15

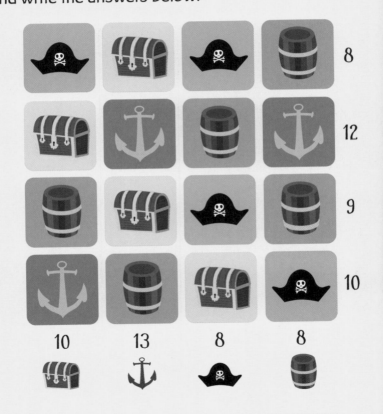

Draw a line between each print in the sand and the boot (or peg leg) that made it.

Circle six differences between these two pictures.

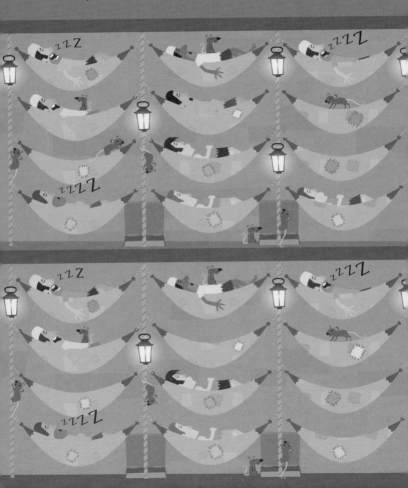

Find these two groups in the treasure below.

Fill in the missing numbers on the sails, so that all three masts add up to the same total.

Find the words below in the grid.

```
A  N  O  T  E  L  E  K  S
F  I  D  L  O  G  U  S  H
C  T  B  S  A  N  D  U  A
O  G  W  E  H  L  A  P  R
R  N  I  R  A  M  Y  O  K
A  U  D  R  E  J  H  T  I
L  B  E  Q  S  C  U  C  M
K  M  U  Z  N  E  K  O  G
E  R  L  A  C  O  D  T  S
```

CORAL	SHARK	GOLD
WRECK	ANCHOR	SAND
OCTOPUS	EMERALDS	SKELETON

How many pirates can be dressed from the items below? Each pirate needs a jacket, shorts, a pair of boots and something to wear on his head.

Fill in the blank squares so that each row, column and block contains all six of the symbols below.

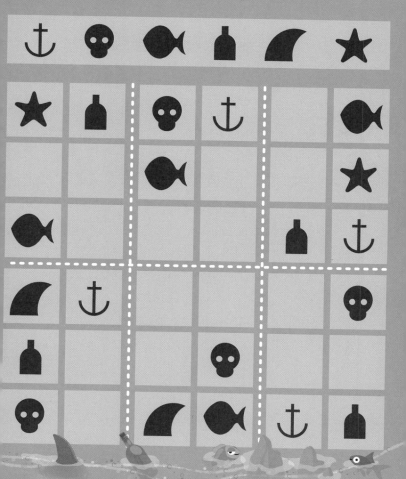

Find the stranded pirate
a route back to his ship
before it sets sail.

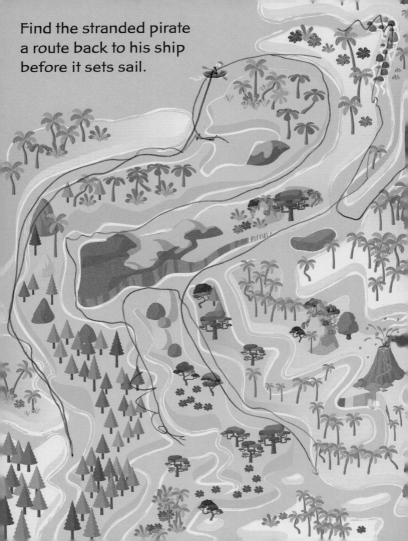

Are there more red or green rings in this picture?

Answers

1 Answer: c

2
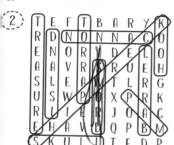

3
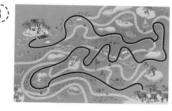

4

5

6

Answers

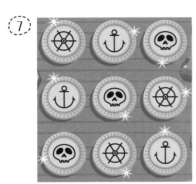

(8) **Answer**: Yes. He'll spend exactly 200 silver pieces.

(9) **Answer**: C

(10)

(13) **Answer**: 1. GOLD, 2. BIRD, 3. WIND, 4. SAND

Answers

(14)

(15)

4 3 1 2

(16)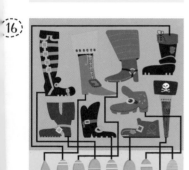

(17)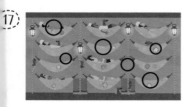

(18)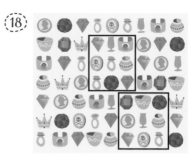

(19)

(20)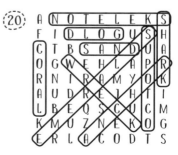

Answers

(21) **Answer:** 7

(22)
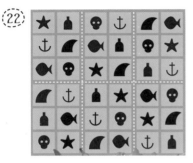

(23)

(24) **Answer:** Red.
17 red rings and
16 green rings

Digital manipulation by Keith Furnival
Edited by Sam Taplin

First published in 2018 by Usborne Publishing Ltd. 83–85 Saffron Hill, London ECIN 8RT, England.
www.usborne.com Copyright © 2018 Usborne Publishing Ltd. The name Usborne and the devices ♀ ⊕ are